More Praise for *gossypiin*

"Ra Malika Imhotep's *gossypiin* presents us with an elixir, blending us with our recent past and our strange present. We can't begin to imagine the emotional and psychic reality of what has happened in the spaces between our current moment and the past 600 years. What we have are records told in breath passed down with love lilting on the tongue like a prayer. What we have are segmented borders and dizzying self-immolating desires sometimes. Imhotep is aware of this and moves us back to breath, back to scars and love poured into the earth. Imhotep acts as Circe, placing our hands into the hands that gingerly unearthed medicinals that gave our Black ancestors autonomy over their bodies. Throughout the book we experience glimpses into how care and joyful sensuality coexist with heartbreak and betrayal, and how these dualities make for creation."
—Jasmine Gibson, author of *Don't Let Them See Me Like This*

"*gossypiin* is an offering to the Black femme flesh that exists in and outside the parameters of gender. The poems in this collection reread the archive of the antebellum era, both the written and the gossiped, to point to the multiple forms of escape that Black femmes and their kin imagined and employed through the use of cotton root. In gossypiin, the American South is recognized as the geography that midwives 'wild wimmin,' Black femme subjects who turn to reinventing themselves as a fugitive practice. It is this shapeshifting that nuances the canon of trans and queer poetics. For Ra Malika Imhotep, Blackness cannot be detached from (un) gendering and transitioning. In fact, the collection proposes that when one moves 'away from / woman,' one will finally arrive 'into the black' / into blk / into wimmin / blk wimmin.' The 'blk wimmin' is the ancestor, relative, and future ancestor who teaches us to 'come back often' to all that is 'soft and *black*.'

"*gossypiin* is a prayer for Black trans, queer, sick, disabled, Southern, and 'girl-born' kin everywhere."
—Alan Pelaez-Lopez, author of *Intergalactic Travels: Poems from a Fugitive Alien*

gossypiin

poems

Ra Malika Imhotep

 Red Hen Press | *Pasadena, CA*

Book design by Mark E. Cull

Cover art by Alison Saar, *High Cotton II*, linocut, published by Mullowney Printing, Portland, Oregon.

Library of Congress Cataloging-in-Publication Data

Names: Imhotep, Malika Ra, author.
Title: Gossypiin : poems / Ra Malika Imhotep.
Description: First edition. | Pasadena, CA : Red Hen Press, [2022]
Identifiers: LCCN 2021029272 (print) | LCCN 2021029273 (ebook) | ISBN
    9781636280257 (trade paperback) | ISBN 9781636280264 (epub)
Subjects: LCGFT: Poetry.
Classification: LCC PS3609.M53 G67 2022 (print) | LCC PS3609.M53 (ebook)
    | DDC 811/.6—dc23
LC record available at https://lccn.loc.gov/2021029272
LC ebook record available at https://lccn.loc.gov/2021029273

The National Endowment for the Arts, the Los Angeles County Arts Commission, the Ahmanson Foundation, the Dwight Stuart Youth Fund, the Max Factor Family Foundation, the Pasadena Tournament of Roses Foundation, the Pasadena Arts & Culture Commission and the City of Pasadena Cultural Affairs Division, the City of Los Angeles Department of Cultural Affairs, the Audrey & Sydney Irmas Charitable Foundation, the Meta & George Rosenberg Foundation, the Albert and Elaine Borchard Foundation, the Adams Family Foundation, Amazon Literary Partnership, the Sam Francis Foundation, and the Mara W. Breech Foundation partially support Red Hen Press.

First Edition
Published by Red Hen Press
www.redhen.org

Acknowledgments

"Rememory" was previously published in *The Breakbeat Poets Vol 2 : Black Girl Magic* Haymarket Books 2018.

"Lil Cotton's First Will and Testament" was commissioned by the artist Andrew Wilson for the opening of his Solo exhibition at The Museum of The African Diaspora in San Francisco, CA. The poem is a response to his piece entitled *Cotton Husk Body*.

"One of Four Women Walking down Peachtree Street Licking Herself" and "Home is a Mouth Full of Spit" were originally published as part of *Scalawag Magazine*'s Poetry and Playlist series.

"mammy-made potion" and "Miss Graham Say . . ." were originally published in the Gender Issue of the online literary publication *Auburn Avenue*.

For the lost one
For the hands and hearts that worked me into being
For the future in the hands and hearts of my nieces, nephews,
niblings, baby cousins and 'nem

For Naveah & Xan & Milani & Cetira & Marley
For D. Makeda Johnson & Akbar Imhotep

Contents

Sow

Seedling

Flower

Fruit

Harvest

gossypiin

Stories Come and Stories Go
Listen to the Words
and Help Them Grow

It Matters Not if the Stories are True
Only What
They Mean to You

'Cause Stories Come and Stories Go
Listen to the Words
and Away We Go!

—Akbar Imhotep, Master Storyteller,
Puppeteer, Puppet Maker

Gossypium herbaceum

Official use: the root bark of this plant was officially recognized in the USP from 1863–1916 for its effects on the uterine organs. In the nineteenth century the active principle was called "gossypiin"

Other Afro-American Use: "In 1840 a French writer, Bouchelle, reported that the root bark of cotton was widely used by Negro slaves in America to induce abortion. According to Johns U. Lloyd, "the credit for the discovery of its uses [as an abortificent] must be given to the Negroes of the South."
—From *Hoodoo Medicine: Gullah Herbal Remedies* by Faith Mitchell

And so, they must've plunged hands deep beneath the field, gently undoing the crop to coax it out of its medicine.

And so, they must've taken it, gingerly in their hands, tucked into waistbands, smuggled into kitchens where it became powder and poultice and tea.

And so, they must've made a place for that which was cast out, a plot to catch their waters: tears, spit, blood, and indignation.

And so, they must've gotten familiar with the inside parts, the space between, before and after invasion.

And so, they must've returned somewhere, dreamt of another place, found themselves on new altars in spaces kin they could only imagine would call home.

What We Gathered Here to Do

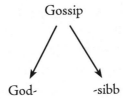

Gossip

God-   -sibb

Part of gossip is the telling of what Zora Neale Hurston and those she surveyed in *Mules and Men* might call *big lies*, what Webster defines as "casual or unconstrained conversation or reports about other people, typically involving details that are not confirmed as being true." Gossipin' passes between those who are related in some divine way be it by blood or porch step. In Middle English a "Gossip" was a confidant, one with whom secrets are shared. This mode of intimate relation between women, who were then seen as property, existed in the space of the mundane, outside of the purview of those who would be Masters. Fearing its potential to upset the order of things, patriarchal logics rushed to denigrate the magic of the exchange.

> This conception of "gossip," as we have seen, emerged in a particular historical context. Viewed from the perspective of other cultural traditions, this "idle women's talk" would actually appear quite different. In many parts of the world, women have historically been seen as the weavers of memory—those who keep alive the voices of the past and the histories of the communities, who transmit them to the future generations and, in so doing, create a collective identity and profound sense of cohesion. —Silvia Frederici[1]

As Hurston wrote in *Moses, Man of the Mountain*, "the female companion of man has the gift of the soothing-balm of lies." Connecting this more prophetic narrative understanding of feminine lies that soothe

---

1   Silvia Federici, "How the Demonization of 'Gossip' Is Used to Break Women's Solidarity," *Inthesetimes* (blog), January 31, 2019, https://inthesetimes.com/article/21707/the-subversive-feminist-power-of-gossip.

to Hurston's elucidation of "big lies" as part of an indispensable canon of Black folklore, the lies of gossip can be seen as a sacred exchange beyond the metrics of merit or value. In *Their Eyes Were Watching God*, when Hurston's protagonist Janie tells her confidant Pheoby, "you can tell 'em what Ah say if you wants to, Dat's just de same as me 'cause my tongue is in mah frien'ds mouf;" she gestures toward an awareness of the centrality of gossip to the community's social life. While Janie and Pheoby go on to decry the need of the town's folk to "put a mouf on things they don't know nothin' about," in the intimacy of their exchange which is the frame of the entire novel's unfolding, Pheoby sits "eager to feel and do through Janie" while Janie leans into her "full of the oldest human longing—self-revelation."[2] I root myself here because in this offering of stories heard, told, repressed, recovered, and imagined I have made the choice to put my tongue in your mouth. I do so, in an effort to say something to somebody about this peculiar inheritance of violation and survival and magic.

Writing about her artistic challenges and discoveries, in the anthology *Moon Marked & Touched by Sun*, writer/performer Robbie McCauley offers that "dialogue is an act." That "saying the words allowing dialogue, making dialogue happen is an act, a useful act in the moment."[3] And so, to this moment of continued concern over the mattering of Black lives and the longstanding contest of power over Reproductive Justice, I engaged in dialogue with myself, my family, my ancestors, my therapist, lovers, friends, and these poems about the experiences carried in my body and the bodies that came before mine. The majority of these poems reflect an internal dialogue between many voices that live inside me. They are all an interruption of narrative silence around sexual trauma and the mark it makes on black femme subjectivity.

---

2   Zora Neale Hurston, *Their Eyes Were Watching God*, Reissue edition (New York, NY, Harper Perennial Modern Classics, 1998), 6–7.

3   "Sally's Rape," in *Moon Marked and Touched by Sun: Plays by African-American Women*, 1st edition (New York, Theatre Communications Group, 1993), 212.

Following McCauley, I am "going against the myth of the romance of the slave master and the overseers with the slave women . . . I'm going against the myth because it was a power thing, so we call it rape. Sometimes it was actual, brutal rape; sometimes it might have been romantic. It doesn't matter."[4] So when I talk about my Great-Great Grandmother Ann Valentine in terms that may seem incongruent to the ways the stories have been passed down in my family it is a decision to look power squarely in the face and in that looking, to offer to my own body a tender space of understanding.

Gossip and Gossypiin are connected at the root. Gossipin' is a trickster technology. Gossipin' is what we do together against better judgement. Gossypiin is what we are. The active principle. I think of *gossypiin* as something in between what Ntozake Shange called a choreopoem and what Audre Lorde named a bio-mythography. It is a Black feminist hypertext that registers the feeling of an experience of the world in which the self is an unstable plurality continuously unmade. It is a story marked into the flesh of the poet, transferred onto the page through a process of distillation shaped by the pedagogy of June Jordan and the interior celebrations of Lucille Clifton. An enactment of Black feminist poetic utterance that tends to the inside parts.

gossypiin relies on the fogginess of memory. *gossypiin* listens between the silence. *gossypiin* abandons absolute truths for the Truth of how history wearsout the black femme body.

Lil Cotton Flower emerges to aid in this act. They are a funky Black feminist fantasy. A character I inhabit on stage to "strip down layers of attenuated meaning." A sticky trickster-self that has emerged from the "marvels of my own inventiveness."[5] In these pages they have revealed themself to me as a playful presence with no investment in being respectable nor human. They

---

4   "Sally's Rape," 214.
5   Hortense J. Spillers, "Mama's Baby, Papa's Maybe. An American Grammar Book," *Diacritics* 17, no. 2 (1987). 67, https.//doi.org/10.2307/464747.

knew the stories before I heard them. They danced out their meanings and waited for me to catch on.

Since this harvest of poems is inspired by the plant medicine latent in *Gossypium herbaceum*, or cotton root bark, the structure of the text loosely follows the cycle of the cotton plant from sowing to harvest. This is also a nod toward the cyclical patterns of knowing, sensing, and healing central to many African and Indigenous epistemologies. The narrative moves with no fidelity to progress.

gossypiin is an invitation to witness the registering of a story still living in and acting on the body, a presence still escaping capture . . .

After and with
Francis Taylor, Ann Valentine, Carrie Lee Davis Ridley, Ira Dean Davis, Lucy Perkins, Susie Moody, Sarah Moody, Rebecca Moody, Makeda Searson Ahad, Queen Elizabeth Graham, Deborah Yahvah, Sharifa Saa Maat & Njeri Willis

Sow

My daddy says I've misremembered. The Big Tree and the women gathered underneath it belonged to the Davises. The church too and the plot with the white graves and the laughing cousins.

Ann Valentine is somewhere else. Her master lay _____ struck under a shared patch of ground way up the road. These Harts ain't easy to understand, let alone keep up with. My own granddaddy was a rumored death until I turned three.

There was a Mother somewhere in Georgia who lost one child to slavery. There was a Mother up North who birthed so many the State would label her a nuisance. Some dark some light. Some Johnsons. Some Perkins.

The Moody women come to me easy. I care for them most days without thinking about it. They run wild up and down the eastern seaboard. My mama brought us back down to where the dirt runs red. I cry enough for the both of us.

I find my self between the fragments. My mind refuse to hold it like it's regular. Seem like I need to mash it up to get the sense out.

Copresence II

great great grand-mammy valentine
takes me back
under

& you
gon' have to leave   or
at least don't touch

this body—
ain't mine,

just some thing they made
time to dig up.

still got dirt on it
that ain't no body bother

to kiss
up to god

_____'s Rape

after Ann Valentine and Robbie McCauley

an excited _____ man caresses a negress
who mothers the children he owns
but this _____ man's love
signs over land
& my daddy's people

                                                    build a church
                                                    in no one's honor.

The negress lays there
                            a cracked cement heart given over
                            to a small forest of neglect
                                            & that's how we know it's her
                                            under the dirt that holds our feet up.

Some nights it's me *down on the ground getting done it to.*
Sometimes it's my own _____ being muffled under some nigga
I thought I dreamed up.

                            Sometimes I forget the texture of my own refusal.
                            Some days I wake up tasting the magic of it.

Ma Dear

a body

                              my body

leaving itself.
A body

                              my body

not feeling
just watching

                              assuming

this is

                              the first time.

A body

                              her body

opening

                              closing itself.

A body

                              her body

enduring.

                              Her body

a body

through

                              which

we all survive/d.

Lil Cotton Flower births themself out
of the forced togetherness of a quiet wound

A con   torted union
   of one Hart   and a Valentine
      marked   me
        coal-color   ed Venus
         love child

daughter of dusky sweet almost.

In her memory, I play
dress up with store brought cotton

branches
give my self   a new
name.
Dance out of my skin
in front of strangers. Fall down

and find my self
crying.

Obscure Origins 2: The Player

Obscure Origins 1: The Sculptor

Lil Cotton Flower sings / them self a song

I play with myself
like a doll. I love being
this thing that come
from out they hands.

I am more imagination
than blood. Prayed into,
prayed over—conjured
on an embattled bridge
between clay and cloth.

I was never baby, only doll.
Pulled out of hands
that don't fit together
except for in the making
of this offering.

I play with myself
to keep the seams
from breaking.

I prey to all
real things.
Their hands

reach toward Me
but I feel for

some thing
else.

Seedling

The first time I heard the story was between cracks of aged linoleum in Aunt Lil's kitchen. I sat uncomfortably southern in the Bronx high rise that held all my mother's secrets, careful to stare only at things that could not look back. Aunt Lil's skin wrinkled around the mucous filled hole in her throat, rippling like water as she rattled into the mechanical voice box insurance had finally paid for.

"you and yo lil' mosquito bite titties" grunted the matriarch.

"hunh?" I, great niece turned granddaughter by the informal structure of the kin-dom, blushed, turning the corner to the bathroom where I would analyze my chest, the nipples and soft flesh around them that I hadn't thought twice about until this trip. I stood there staring at the subtle hint of what's supposed to be "woman" not knowing what to make of it. Soon my mother knocked on the door with a comforting giggle.

"If you think Aunt Lil is bad you should meet Shirley!" I did not get the joke but accepted the warmth of my mother's humor. Smiling hesitantly, I opened the door and followed her back into the kitchen.

My mother walked to the stove and leaned out the window. The wind in her face woke her to memory. My focus followed her, staring hard as to not ever, not even for a moment, let my eyes wander to Aunt Lil and the hole left by her tracheotomy. Still facing the wind, My mother gets to talking about a boy . . .

after mama sighs
real heavy. Her eyes pools of
scarred ivory.   I search
her face for wet and see pupils held
in corneal arca the color of ocean.

exile in pursuit of the New South

When my mother moved to Georgia
the elders rolled their eyes
in protest. Ain't she know
better? Couldn't she feel
the bothersome heat
of that hostile soil?

Why give a good womb
over to that dirt?

Grandma Sarah's maiden name was Moody. I wore it around my neck
in 14 karat gold until the chain broke. A totem marking me theirs. I felt
like I needed her close to me. Like I needed to see her in the mirror, but
the truth is I've always seen out through her eyes. Maybe it was Rebecca
Moody who found me there. The great aunt I've only seen in archives: the
one photo where she smiles next to an Egyptian bust and the one line in
her father's census record from before she left Georgia. Rebecca's memory
helps my mother make sense of me. And Grandma Sarah, or the stories
I've been told about her—throwing parties, dancing, drinking, laying
naked on the floor under the ceiling fan—help me make sense of it all.

Wild Wimmin Don't Worry

for Aunt Rebecca who may very well have invented herself

ain't no time
to sit 'round weepin
when there's a family coming
up behind you

and the cheeks of Italian men
need kissing. Palms greasy
sliding up and around
the numbers ledger

the lovers come as they may
and fit to my liking. *Hot and hard
and soft all at the same time*—ain't no
need to fuss over what
to call it when it feels good
and the bills is paid.

My mother dreams

Her mother is in the hospital and I, who was born four months after her death, put 20 dollars on her cell phone so my mama could speak with her. Mama calls the hospital and they say Grandma Sarah ain't got no phone. Mama is raising hell with the nurses when she wakes up and calls me.

Grandma Sarah ain't finish the seventh grade. Had my mama at sixteen. My grandfather was a grown man, twice her age. But he loved his little Diane. He died in a fire when my mother was thirteen. I don't know how to miss him but I see his absence in my mother's eyes. At my college graduation, Aunt Shirley slaps my thigh to tell me how good my color is. Color deep like her brother George.

My mama was the type of daughter who would cry every time her father fixed himself to leave for work. Cried so much he lost that job. Aunt Shirley say she was supposed to take in my mother after her brother died but mama went to Aunt Lil in the Bronx. Aunt Lil passed when I was in middle school. At the funeral, I cried into everyone's face.

They never look at me without talking about Sarah's eyes.

earth bound

gettin' black as i want
which is a ruddy shade of deep
brown, which is the color
of the clay i am born
of. my mama
sculpts a face into the mound
and i watch and i wonder
if she be god.

my god for whom hell
is an anxious spiral,
a back ache, a leg cramp
and heaven the nursed hands
that massage it back to feeling.

she cry out and i wait too long
to see if she serious
make my way down
stairs to see her
hurting and in this touch
we share something
holy. hands pressed into flesh

tryna bring ease.
in the return of care
i find myself
breathless
and awestruck

how its my hands now
tending the earth colored
body. bringing it life.

A Question of Attunement

my mama say she in love now
and something leaves me
wet-faced and wanting

empty-faced, hollowed
hysterical—mama, but
if you need love how
can i need anything but?

this man
his hands
on you making you anew

something more than
mama, but i need you
still, unchanging pillar of
wait mama, but—love?

how it feel? can you teach me this time?

love and the things two bodies do
to make it ain't nothing
we ever touched on
i mean you and me mama, but
you know i breathe next to lovers in bed
the way i learned next to you?

i'm saying, i hear you mama, but—the breathing
is it how you make love?
is that what we been doing this whole time?

this man, do he breathe
with you? can you feel his chest rising
and falling in time
with yours? it's magic, i think
mama, but—sometimes it work too well.

Where did i think i was going?
giving lovers pieces of what i got from you
wondering why they suckle so hard
and now you here weaning me off and out
your bed and i ain't ready

mama, but this love thing you in
now, it can hurt—you know that?
yes the hurt
i'm born of
that man, my father
the void he left—or opened
that place you fell in and now you say
you out?

                                        can i follow?

Flower

I ain't know when I laid down on the floor crying out for my Grandmothers to come in and help me in this healing that Francis Taylor was classified as a breeder. I ain't know her daughter, my Great-Grandmother, Susie Moody narrowly escaped forced sterilization by following her oldest daughter Rebecca up north to the apartment they all shared. I ain't know about the nervous breakdowns and maladaptive coping mechanism in my blood. I just knew I needed to hear their voices, to feel their hands.

endurance

I am dry
under the body
busy working
it's way to some place
unfamiliar
yet somehow
inside me.

Hear me,
the wet body
is not mine
it belongs
to the other.

See me—
passive opening,
mouthing anguish,
dry and elsewhere.

My body
down there,
the body
over me
raining its salt
into my mouth.

A taste
I enjoy
to spite
the ache

the hermit-woman takes a lover

after gayl jones

i am a woman/generous/with place and things/stingy/with time and soul/except for
this/stranger
and so it goes/ i throw my flesh/ into your mouth,
watch you chew/ with wide-eyes
most times i am thrilled/ others i forget
to breathe/and in/this stifled/ presence/ i leave/ my body
as i've/ been trained/to do/and wait
for you/ to finish/so that i/ may rest/again

Some nights talking to god and talking to pussy bleed into each other.

I grope my self in search of ovaries and sometimes feel something
but most nights it's no groping just a laying on of my own hands
tryna conjure all the sorrow
out the song

somebody forgot to tell somebody something

"Particularly the women. What women say to each other and what they say to their daughters is vital information, that's education. It's not gossip, it's not girl talk, it's information . . . And they either have to discover it for themselves, and through incredible amounts of trauma, or they have to invent themselves . . ."
—Toni Morrison in conversation with Ntozake Shange (1978)

5

What do you do when the blood stops early?

4

When i become this weeping needing thing? This deep breathing wet-faced monster of my self? What kinda swamp i don' dug myself out of? How i get here? How this hurt here? How a chest tighten itself into pumped fist?

3

Who taught me how to love half empty? In what language did i first learn to plead for closeness? How did Grandma Sarah spell out her lonely? What kinda pot she cook it in? Did my mother watch? Might there be a recipe book up underneath the bed?

2

Where do we go to hum out these bones? Is there a stretch of muscle that sings in the right key? How i'mma get there? When i'mma get my license? Will they let me rest tonight?

1

What sound you supposed to make when it's over? How did you know you've arrived? What else might surrender mean? How often do you change the sheets?

amenorrhea

spirits smack talk up
and down my spine asking
for shit in languages
I can't hear yet

& all I can offer is a wet face.
the wound burrows itself
across the mound they mark
"reproductive"

& the mirror prays too, my breast held
out like communion—take, eat, this
is the body broken for you

& I wish it was that easy,
I've pretended often
a mouth latch on
to suck and I'll moan out
some sort of mantra, some thing
they need

& they leave or get boo'd off
the stage this bed has become

& somehow I'm standing there holding
the broom that pushed 'em and feeling
satiated 'cept for the reflection
of my own shea buttered hands
offering up nipples the circumference

of a sunflower's heart
petals wilting

& there can't be nothin' honey
bout this 'cause it taste rotten

& I thought
it was our secret.
you keep whispering
and I hold all the blood

& let the lining clot to leather, press
my hand to the ache and breathe, make nice
with the heaviness, serve it
room temperature water
and herb soaked menstruum

& for all this ceremony
I'm still standing over the kitchen sink
phantom lips to my back
hands greased in other niggas waste
wonderin'   maybe the rest comes
without permission

anovulatory or fugitivity at the meeting place of my thighs

what sent her running?

all of it

come together and held in this body
a little too much to carry
and keep on with nature as usual
so she followed her own North Star and got gone
somewhere

like Black Moses got her
shotgun pressed
to the nape of her neck
she leave me here
inspecting all my waters

the moon rises full and new
and draws no blood

i scroll myself into
a ledger of panic

then set a new course:

bad womb
is wound
is handed to me by mother
is the miracle I birthed myself out of
is my body's refusal
is my invitation away from
               woman
                    into beyond
                       into the black
                       into blk
                           into wimmin
                             blk wimmin
                             is we
                             is co-created against time
                             is the miracle
                             is the refusal
                             is the invitation

**the poet stares longingly into a black queer elsewhere
and feels themself unravel**

after a 2014 production of Sharon Bridgforth's River See

> He ain't let me say "yes" the first
> time, but now they ain't
> got no choice.

> this my body now.

> That nigga ain't never touch me
> nowhere
> deep as the everything
> found in the wet dark
> of her mouth.

I have forgotten how to speak
this mourning. I am still the dead
thing left down there beneath the boy
playing god, drunk off his own power.

The love I want to make is trapped
inside a body disfigured by an event
I cannot name, and now rest eager for its own
disappearance. I hear: "Sick ain't sick,
it's god talkin' to ya" and ache
toward some less lonely
version of my self.

> Seem like there's something Ida about learning
> to document my suffering:

~~I love you, but he took it and now I have nothing to offer~~
~~but absence.~~

I hate how dire it sounds
whenever I write it. I hate how muddy it gets
when you in the after tryna love your own who and how and
when . . .

Dreams of the dead thing I was mistaken for
don't make the living less lonely.

But watching See, I find her tongue in my mouth.
And remember to keep moving toward my inevitable,
to make of these moments
choices toward that place where love finds me / naked
and happy like before I decided
to be born.

madrigal para las vientres negras

after Nicolas Gullien

my womb knows more than my mind
as much as my thighs
the true grace of my naked black body

slicks the sheets with shea butter and sweat
marked by the jungle
i breathe with my mouth open

ancient waters run out my eyes
into the mouths of the devout

**Notes toward the integration of a traumatic event
or the scene of my own subjection**

When it was my body
getting done it to

there was no water
beneath the boy I mistook

depersonalization
for magic

I even thanked him
for making me

the impossible—
a woman.

I closed myself up
to indulge a fantasy / of belonging.

Silly girl-born child,
the only thing belonged to

is tradition. Wasn't the first
and despite prayer

won't be the last
of invade territories.

Body a would-be ledger
of control and discipline

Flesh some thing-in-between
and always has been.

Listen, the women who bear
to remember won't let us

forget our rape is a nonevent
like Freedom

No, that's somebody else talking—
It happened and I believe

But did you mean to say
it like that? Do you dare name

a _____ man responsible?
listen, when it was my body

down there beneath the boy
love succumbed. Power

unmade me in the belly
of my foremothers—

How many of us held supine
and called crazy? It takes

a crime to mark criminal
and a subdued negress

is the expected fodder
of this exchange

ain't a thing here
to be redressed.

more than that kind of legibility
I need to sound it out
in my own time. Fix my lips
round words like *harm* and *survivor*

but still keep breathing
deep, deeper

Miss Graham tells my younger self a blue joke

(or a Praisesong for Janie's Pear Tree)

"one day the children asked
why grandma always sittin
on the porch with her legs wide-open
and the grown folks answered
she keepin the flies off her watermelon"

and i can see her
clutching her knees in a fit
of laughter, her lips curled
to smile, her eyes coy
in their gentle humor.

i laugh before understanding
the joke—this funk,
the open-legged bait,
grandma's body a living thing
its organisms courting
other bodies.

a sweet lure
protecting her fruit.

i sit between open legs,
other fingers greasing my parts

i inhale deep and don't say nothin'

                    whole black seeds slip
                  out the side of my mouth
                new laughter buzzing about
                            my knees

to memory I pray a poem
to meet my
baby cousins and 'nem
before the shame

before the too harsh scrubbing
and blistered skin, before callous
and the simple invasion of disgust

before the snickers and side long glances
before she learns herself the disquieting odor
of a bradford pear tree

                    let there be *the panting breath*
            of the breeze, the dust-bearing bee sunk
                    into the sanctum of a bloom,
            the ecstatic shiver from root to branch.

                        Let there be truth
                    funky like how we grow
                            to like it

                    Let there be a Mama
                      who ain't afraid
                            to tell it

mammy-made potion

after Nambi E. Kelley's Jazz, *after Toni Morrison's* Jazz

violet spreads herself crimson
between the legs of a young promise

no babies

just city slick sweet talk
and the rushed plummet of a chosen love.
daughter-aged girl

hot beneath her sash
chasin' death right out
an old woman's bed

and here, the would-be baby
falls into a suspension, a less than nothing
saturating the chest of annoyed lovers

and in the Change ain't no more
choice. mother hunger rolls itself
out from behind memory

a daughter's longing to forget
the mothers body cramped
in the damp narrow of a well

bleeding into all the water.

Fruit

Da Peach Squad

for Tiara, Tina, Deranda, Mironda, Monica , & Lena

I.

One summer half the girls in my middle school class moved into my house
and worked at a neighborhood summer camp spending our days and nights
traversing the nook of West Atlanta to which I belong. Watching Nu-Nu
and 'dem pop their lips to our rhythms in *ATL* inspired us to become a crew
and practice dance routines for weekend lock-ins at *Cascade Skating Rink*.

But we spent more time that summer smelling ourselves, getting cute and
creating our own drama.

One night when my cousins were in town from East New York we sat
around socializing in my backyard with some young and relatively harmless
niggas who were poised to flee at first sign of my mother's headlights. I don't
remember what happened but things went left.

II.

My oldest cousin pulled rank and declared the party—done.

I, being rambunctious and with a rep to prove, resisted.

A door was locked.

Someone hopped in a window.

III.

the next day fear and embarrassment unfurled
across my face
hard.

& maybe I spent that afternoon mourning my own social death, cried myself
to sleep and woke into flesh
& maybe that was when I first lost my body.

One of Four Women Walking Down Peachtree Street Licking Herself

after Nina Simone

Nina dredged up Peaches
from the back of her throat

let it out with a sonic break
I lose myself in
over and over again

Auntie Linda say
when you heard her sing it
you could feel it
and knew
exactly who she was talking 'bout

You could see her,
Bitter-Black daughter of slaves
hiding sweetness under tar-colored callous

manner tough like fist balled
tight as a heart
held before her chest
like a prayer she scared
to have answered

and Southern as I am
I still like my peaches unripe—
like when the flesh resist
my teeth a lil bit

or at least that's what I thought I liked,
till one day I bit hard

and felt the sweet of it slip
through my fingers right
down my arm

and before I could think
my tongue went chasing after it
and right then the brown
wasn't bitter no more

just soft like how I imagine
molasses feel to spoon
or less metal—like honey
to comb

and my hand still held the too-soft flesh
and the sun coming down
made it shine something like special
and my mouth start to get sticky hot
with all that sugar turning molasses.

I let out a thick smile
and seen Nina smirking
in the back of my mind

fingering the piano
with enough force to shake the sugar
out the trees

I mean

the peaches all fall when she start singing
they hit the ground and roll all over themselves, spent.

some get stepped on
others picked up
and ate on
or forgotten on the counter
till they start to eat away at themselves

And that's what I'm doing
eatin' away at my self

a mouth full of home dripping
down my arm
walking down this new street

toward the new place i call home
and the magic of it

is right here

in the back of my throat

Lil Cotton Flower Tells a Story

Before freedom and again 400 years into its afterlife, Brer Fox grabbed up some tar and turpentine and let me make myself through his hands.

Grinning and feeling all accomplished he surrendered to this muse. You see, the morning i came to him, Brer Fox was out to get the best of that ol' Brer Rabbit—the quick moving trickster always pullin' the wool over Brer Fox, Brer Bear and even Ol'Massa.

Payin' them no mind, i made use of Brer Fox's ol' hands and fix'd myself up real nice and round in all the right places: two pearls through which to see, a wood button for a nose, a thick red slash of lip—all set into the soft blackness of my face.

i whisper'd into that ol' Fox's ear to dress me up nice and alluring, and he fetch a few spools of yarn to weave atop my head and set me down right at the lip of the river where as i can watch the water glitter. little did he know, this here water is my Ma Dear. She the only one i answer too.

While i settle into my prettiness, Brer Fox look on and commence to singing to himself about the rabbit he finna catch on my account and what a nice dinner that meat'll make once it meet his eatin' plate.

And so's i just sit there, lookin' out at the water, havin' deep conversations his ears ain't pitched to catch. Thanking Ma Dear for letting me take form this evening. Not paying much mind to the Fox but thanking him for his hands all the same.

Then trot up that ol' Brer Rabbit—moving so fast he almost missed this lil' ol' black thing sitting at the river's edge.

At the sight of that Rabbit, Brer Fox jump under the bush cross the road and hide

Then Brer Rabbit pause, double back and give me a deep glance over—lookin' real close with some secret heat behind his eyes. First Brer Rabbit get to talm 'bout how i'm is a "sassy ol' Jay bird"

and I'm almost flattered 'cept for that flame in his eye tell me to keep to myself.

Brer Rabbit commence to getting awfully familiar. He say "hey there, *Brown Sugar* how 'bout you let me have a lick at yo sweetness!" and my Tar Baby self just sits there, ain't sayin' nothin'—Brer Fox still tucked away under the bush, softly humming his eatin' song as he watch.

Brer Rabbit say "okay now! *Earth Mama* why don't you bend over and carry my load" Tar Baby ain't sayin' nothin' and Brer Fox, he lay low.

Brer Rabbit keep searching for a name I'm primed to respond to, he seem to speak from a list that start off calm but then grow indignant: alright then *Peaches?* He grumbles . . . how 'bout it *Sapphire?*, oh you must think you *God's Holy Fool?*—

"'How you come on, den?" Brer Rabbit, ask . . . gettin' big mad.
Tar Baby stay still, en Brer Fox, he lay low.

Brer Rabbit fix his mouth to say, "black as I is, my nose up so high I caint even smell my own breath"

Say he got something to fix me. And I'm just there, ain't sayin' nothin' as the sun heat me up into softness.

Brer Rabbit puff up his chest and says: "I'mma learn you how to talk to a respectable man like me if it's the last act of this here show" And I don't know who he think he talkin' to but being the Tar Baby I am, I keep my mouth shut. Sitting pretty. Getting soft in all the right places.

Brer Rabbit yelling now. He say, *"Cain't you hear me calling you, miss honey? Or is you as dumb as you is black? If you don't fix yo' face and greet me imma bus' you wiiiiiide open"*

& Ain't much of nothing for me to do in the face of no madrabbitnigga so I just stay still. Wondering if Brer Fox still watching, i can't hear him humming no more . . .

Brer Rabbit keep on yelling . . .

Tar Baby, keep on sayin' nothin' . . .

Then that niggarabbit draw back his fist and it land right upside my head where the sun been kissin' and he get stuck. He try to grab at my neck and that hand get stuck too. He kick his legs up right at the *di space between* my legs. He yanking and pulling and twisting just getting' more tied up in my sticky mess of a body.

In the struggle I commence to melt 'round myself and it look like we dancing in a pool of molasses.

& I aint never say nothin'

"If you don't let me loose" he shout "I'mma kick the natal stuffing outta you" I don't say nothin' but I think deep about where I was befo all dis. In the dark wet warmth of Ma Dear's belly. The natal stuff I used to swim in. that which this here rabbit is tryna beat out of me.

& I ain't say nothin'

Then here come that ol' fox talm 'bout "Howdy Brer Rabbit . . . you look sorta stuck up this mawnin'"

Brer Fox laugh and laugh and laugh. Laugh Like he done forgot how I moved through his hands this morning. What a pretty thing I made myself before he trotted me out for some Rabbit meat.

Right as the turpentine start to drip out the round of button hole of my eyes, Ma Dear, the river, rear up real big flooding the marsh. She grab me from off the log and start to mixing her sweet waters all around that rabbit and I.

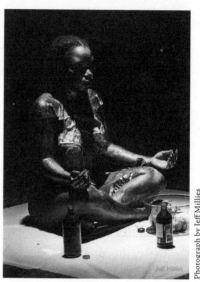

Figure 1
Ra Malika Imhotep as Lil Cotton Flower,
October 2019

Soon I am loosed from him. Loosed from the slug of flesh that held him and I together.

Soon I give up my self in a dark warmth, the color of tar.

And Ma Dear say, "Baby, I tried to told bout messing with these skinfolks. They don't know how to hold something soft and black as you. Next time be sure to fix yourself with teeth to smile and a tongue sharp enough to cut."

Mammy Councils Her Kin

Chile,

Let me tell you
'bout these
white folks:

they mostly half-baked
hence the doughy
pallor of skin
mistaken in
lazy comparison
to porcelain.

Don't you worry
your tarred heart none
'bout ways to manage them
and they antics.

No chile, you listen:
it ain't yo duty
to turn back on the oven.
They gon' find they end
they way.

And see, you can trust me
'cause I is yo mammy
meaning I be the one
who birthed in you

something that knows
how to turn pleasure
out of barrenness. Yes chile,
you go on and play a good
negress. But we, we know
how to do them
trickster thangs.

I say you
my Sweet
little picaninny
Ananse. You
a bunch of black
thangs pulled across water.
Eight legs of my know how
Spread branch-like
come back in all
that we call body, in all
that skin wraps 'round.

What's that you ask?
How you s'posed to breathe? Chile,
aint you minding what I'm fixing
my mouth to say?

You got a life in you
that don't need no lungs. Hell!
barely need flesh.

I

Keep that heart beating
long as I see fit and
can't no heavy footed
so-called "white man"
do a damn thing
about it!

Home is a mouth full of spit for your tender heart

I.
The humidity moves into
my skin
and breaks up all my English

the words start drippin'
from one to the next
seem like my tongue get fatter
when I'm back home
won't move 'round fast enough,
can't pick up the right syllable

just lounge around my mouth
pooling up too thick saliva
I spit out the side my face
like all the niggas
I used to watch
pose 'round the corner store

and all the niggas that came before them
who shot craps against that same wall
talking shit like it's syrup

a young black thing,
pretty like me, walk by
and that spit turn to steam
creep up the back
of thighs that wouldn't
normally be exposed this time of year

but this a Georgia winter
and when my mama first moved down here,
Sagittarius as she is, they barbecued
on her birthday

all that New York just melted away
and her English started to break too

soon she start to movin' like them
Augusta women, her folks ran north
to get away from

II.
In the kitchen we laugh through a joke
'bout how i'm sounding
like i'm back on somebody plantation

and she let on that she notice
but say that whenever I do decide to speak   English
I speak it good

so good she turn to dictionary
tryna follow where I'm going

say, I be
using them words
in new ways, with new folks
rules

then come home
and melt all them semantics
into something slow
and sloppy and in my voice
I remember stories
that ain't all the way mine

III.
How everything I know
about sound and poem
come from up out
red clay and get stuck
underneath my tongue.

How we wash the headstones
white with our mouths full
of laughter.

And ain't that how we mourn?

How my daddy's sister
used to keep dolls on her bed
just like I do.

And ain't that how you put beauty to rest?

How they used to fill
cuts with cobwebs.

And ain't that where all the wisdom
come from?

How spit is good enough medicine
for anything on the surface.

And ain't that why it pool up
at healing time?

Harvest

my mama tells a story of my great aunt lizzie's funeral during which she held baby-me in her arms as she approached the casket to caress the cold cheek of her beloved—and baby-me watching all this feeling—baby-me knowing my mother as a sculptor—baby-me knowing Barbie as a portable best friend—said "mommy, I wanna play with the doll too"

Second Trimester

Aunt Rebecca died

six-weeks later

Grandma Sarah died

four-months later

I was born

Grandma Sarah mourns her only son

The man I was 'posed to love   most   ain't live   past
his crawling. Left   right after   making it out
of me.   Almost like it was   a
mistake.

Every now   and then   I get to feeling   for him.   So
I go over to the drawer   where I keep his things and   hold them up
to my nose   while the iron heats up.   My oldest watch me   But
don't know   this too   is a crying out.

My arm pressing   the hot metal into   the cotton. Warm
with the life   worked into it   by my arm
that once held the baby boy   barely crawling   to his death.

I been beaten, yeah—and I beat back   most nights   but Roy Jr.
was 'posed to grow   into a man   I could love
the   right   way.

And when I get to feeling   for him,   I let the iron work
warmth into his things.   Then press the memory   to my body

and sing   us both   to sleep.

Copresence I

ain't gotta talk much to feel.

grief leak up the throat and glue
the lips shit sometimes, sometimes the story tell itself
best inside my head, sometimes ain't no word.
sometimes i be every place
but here and ain't no spell
enough to conjure a me
into a now

grief-borne power

that morning ain't smell like the box of chocolates mama had left on the counter. i was furrowed brow stomping toward the kitchen. chest heavy like i couldn't remember the last time i told my mother i loved her.

auntie with the loud mouth and the hard hands, now hairless skin-fitted skeleton, smile propped up against hospital pillow, cup by her side to catch spit. she laughed like recovery, like health, like happy.

mama was well-worn with worry. the kind of bitter that comes when you've been steeped past the point of sweetness. familial ailments multiplying faster than we could honey them. nothing went down easy. we were all friction and forced empathy. all tears in the counselor's office and disappointing report cards. all overwhelmed and preoccupied with everything beyond our control.

i had concluded that the only remedy was in remission or death. stirred my sentiments in with the morning tea. watched from the door as mother sipped. the phone rang. the receiver hurled stones at the windows of her eyes. i watched as she broke.

i knew.

told myself i thought too loud. too selfishly. that grown folks and god shared metaphysical terrain and i shouldn't have meddled where they never intended me to be.

no one ever said "your aunt has breast cancer." no one said "your aunt is sick."

so I slide between their silences and spent four years holding myself responsible for her death.

When prompted I remember

a gaping whole

a butter knife raised to my own wrist

no blood
but the sigh
of my mama's heart
breaking

her arms tight around my shoulders

crying on the kitchen floor

Overstimulated

I don' gave away all the laughter
and love I could smuggle up North
out my mouth.
The only sound that feels right is Miles'
fingers threading the valves
of his favorite lover.
Maybe I'll let his horn beat
this sorrow out of me.
Coax me up some new feelings
and slap them 'cross
my face till I hum

Dispatch from a writing workshop in 2015 in which I am the only nigga alive

for Olga Broumas

Law totes loaded gun like trident, walks heavy.
I see ripples in the face of every black
thing I dare to love. I see temporary

quake of life. I see ricochet, glass breaks.
Something falls apart. Me
this time. No more, nothing, not even

to mourn for, just more waves and splash
against the waters that protect

you. And I just sit, desert against wind
tryna save some me for the morning.
And you can't hear that over laugh,

through the smokey lung, you
have chosen what I can't
seem to avoid. Death, pulling

all that black into your body. Say it relieves
stress, say you do it even when sick.
Can't see how sick I am and how this black

don't pull off. Don't puff up. Don't get me high,
just leave me down here tryna think pretty, tryna be
Light, tryna color words in June.

I think watermelon, cool and sweet and joke—
and something my black makes dirty, makes
mockery. Wonder if Light ever feel this heavy

Wonder if ya'll can smell how much of me
dies off to fit.

all the blk things cry sometimes

see, I aint never really wanted   to die just disappear
for a little while. be   without body   without weight   without
consequence

wonder
what more there is   to specter than scapegoat
what might I feel   if free
is feeling still   a blk thing

am I ever less   than the nothing i've been
handed
how might I break   open the mourning
in my chest   throw the towel in   give up
resign   to the feeling

of air against open   palm
an imagined caress   lightly kissed   open

that's how i want to touch   you,
right   in the place you conjure   me
let's swear   solemnly to be up   in a no good
approximation of my worth   no more
bids at visibility   don't see me
i beg   let me rest
in peace be still be silent be tears muffled
in asphalt be the ground be beneath you

walk on over   spit a crude blessing   pour some of yourself out
for a dead hoe   that looks a little bit like me but goes   by
another name   me dying me needing to get out this body

ain't even gotta stop breathing ya'll, listen

just let this body be
apart from me   something different   maybe
my own thing   do my own thing   let me feel   for once   free

will you miss me?

Copresence IV

i can't introduce you to my people
ain't no shame just shhhh . . .
can't you see we dancing through it ?

need quiet, need calm, need alone

so make like ghost and open the door
while my back turned. leave and don't let me stop you

i promise most times

i don't know

what i want.

This ain't quite memorial

for Kenneka, Nia, Tee Tee, Chynal, Kayla, Toyin & all our kin

the heaviness in my chest knows
safety an illusive myth
every reflection in this world
is a ghost

A girl is gone and I see myself
in the shine on her lips.
She was perhaps less jaded.
Or more daring. or thrown to risk
without choice. But she is gone
all the same and I feel the absence
of her smile in the way
my bed refuses to let go
each mourning.

rememory

My body soft
fresh milled cotton.
A deep brown of dried
blood stain.

    Stumbling into
    the spots
    blood spilled into my
    internet. Look up

    on the train, I'm in
    Fruitvale.
    Can hear the protest of asphalt
    that know it ain't
    made for mausoleum.

    In Brooklyn, I follow
    Cousin up dark
    "Pink Houses" stairway.
    Grab my chest,
    try to catch Akai's
    last breath. Cousin
    already at the door,
    ain't look back
    or think twice. This
    where she live.

Here
I am, blood

blackened body.
All up in other
niggas memories
on accident.

If I cried every time
I stood where some
body colored like
mine lost life
don't think I'd be soft

no more. Think
I'd dry up.
No time

for the little
joy I find pressed
against a body
that ain't dead
yet.

Just salted fault lines
down my face,
cracks in the fullness
of my lips

And what then
will they call me

but dirt.

Lil Cotton Flower's First Will and Testament

Bury me under some shit
that shine good
and black. Make memorial
out of that dusty crop.
Make relic
out of that which pricked
and bled these hands
to callous.

Make gentle offerings.
Dress yourself
in a cool white cloth—
call it cotton, call it king
chew the root and call yourself
holy
or whore
or uppity negress, daughter of field niggas
who died with open mouths
or all that is black and whole
at the bottom of the sea
where we make our *residence*
time and time again.

Please don't call it a grave,
say resting place. Don't lip death
just open mouth to exhale "transition"
let me be
still, and taste a peace
kept from our kind.

How much you think blk wimmin worth
when they lay down and get stuck there?

Don't think too hard, you know the answer—
Listen, I ain't got nothing more
to tell you but to dress yourself
in my honor.

Adorn the hands, honey the skin.
Bring me offerings of polished copper
and whatever stones best throw back the light.

Let a dance ring out from the diamond
meeting place of your thighs. Give each cheek
over to its own resonance. Smell yourself moist
and welcoming in the busyness of this release.

Stomp hard enough to wake up
all them ol' haints you claim as kin. Wail
out a deep joy. Wet your face
with our common salt.

Call this ritual.

Come back often.

The [negress] offers a feather-bed resistance. That is, we let the probe enter, but it never comes out. It gets smothered ~~under a lot of laughter and pleasantries~~.
—Zora Neale Hurston, *Mules and Men*

Credits

The italicized line in "____'s Rape" comes from Robbie McCauley's 1989 performance of "Sally's Rape."

The italicized line in "wild wimmin don't worry" comes from the introduction to Audre Lorde's *Zami: A New Spelling of My Name.*

The italicized lines in "notes toward the integration of a traumatic event . . ." come from June Jordan's "Poem about My Rights." This poem also references concepts from Bessel van der Kolk's *The Body Keeps the Score,* Saidiya Hartman's *Scenes of Subjection,* and Hortense Spillers's "Mama's Baby, Papa's Maybe: An American Grammar Book."

The italicized lines in "the hermit-woman takes a lover" come from Gayl Jones's poem "Stranger" in her collection titled *The Hermit-Woman.*

The title "somebody forgot to tell somebody something" comes from a response given by Toni Morrison in a 1978 interview with Ntozake Shange for *American Rag.*

The closing stanza in "Amenorrhea" references a scene in Toni Morrison's *Beloved.*

"See learns to say yes" references Sharon Bridgforth's theatrical jazz performance installation "River See."

"madrigal para las vientres Negras" is a millennial Black feminist interpretation of one of Nicolás Guillén's madrigals from *Sóngoro cosongo* (1931). This specific madrigal was translated by Robert Marquez and printed in a 1972 issue of the *The Black Scholar.*

The italicized lines in "Miss Graham Say" come from Zora Neale Hurston's *Their Eyes Were Watching God.*

The italicized lines in "Lil Cotton Flower Tells a Story" reference Moi Renee's 1992 single "Miss Honey" along with the first page of Hortense Spillers's "Mama's Baby, Papa's Maybe: An American Grammar Book."

Gratitude

I can only speak for myself. But what I write and how I write is done in order
to save my own life. And I mean that literally. For me literature is a way of
knowing that I am not hallucinating, that whatever I feel/know is.
—Barbara Christian, "The Race for Theory," 1987

This book was written in the spirit of knowing "that whatever I feel/know is."
These poems were written and gathered across space and time as I became
increasingly aware of the particular traumas my bodymind was holding and
how those traumas related to those carried by my foremothers. This was a
dizzying and vulnerable labor that often left me staring into the computer,
my journal, or up at the ceiling completely raw with emotion. I am thankful
that Kate Gale of Red Hen Press saw in this collection a story worth
sharing, and I'm grateful for the team at Red Hen Press for their grace and
steadfastness, even as the world became increasingly unstable. I'm grateful
for Allison Saar who granted me permission to use *High Cotton II* as the
face of this work.

And I'm grateful for any and everyone who took the time to touch it, read it,
hear it, feel it.

This book would not be imaginable without the love, support, and
abundance of memories poured into me by my parents D. Makeda Johnson
and Akbar Imhotep and the active network of ancestors who hold us up in
grace and continue to fan the creative spark we share. This book would not
be imaginable without all my blood-relations; I can't name you all, but I feel
you and hope you feel me too (that includes folks like Asha and Morgan who
may not be blood but have grown with me through it all).

This book would not be imaginable without that one day I sat in a repurposed
Oakland Sanctuary littered with pages from *Their Eyes Were Watching God*
and listened to Rev. Marvin K. White wonder out loud about how the Black
women who came before us might have learned to shut their bodies down in

the face of serial rape and other violations of mindbodyspirit they endured during slavery and in its wake. How miraculous it was that I was, at the time, enrolled in an herbalism course at Ancestral Apothecary and learning about cotton root bark. This book would not be imaginable without those women and femmes in that herbalism course who witnessed me through grief and revelation. This book would not be imaginable without the kin I have found along the way in Atlanta, Waltham/Boston, Berkeley, Oakland, New Orleans, London, and Ghana. This book would not be imaginable especially without my beloved Alan Pelaez Lopez, who never once let me forget that I was an artist and served as my doula throughout this process, encouraging me to collect all the bits and pieces of poems I had sprinkled across the internet and my hard drive and to call it a manuscript. You were the loving hand and stern voice of Black radical poetic experimentation throughout this birth. This book would not be imaginable without the encouragement of Ariel Ward and Christine Board and all the beautiful Black women I have met through their spacemaking work as "exhale collective." This book would not be imaginable without the generous attention of Chiyuma Elliot, who was the first person to edit the manuscript when it was raw. This book would not be imaginable without the semester I spent working with Aya De Leon as the Graduate Student Instructor for June Jordan's legacy course at UC Berkeley, Poetry for The People. This book would not be imaginable without the careful ear of Brandi Catanese, who put me on to the anthology *Moon-Marked and Touched by The Sun* where I found Robbie McCauley. This book would not be imaginable without the UC Berkeley Department of African American Studies, my interdisciplinary academic home.

This book would not be imaginable without the critical play, exploration, and fellowship of The Church of Black Feminist Thought that have allowed me to be further shaped by the many urgent voices of radical Black feminist world-making. I am particularly grateful to my co-convener Miyuki Baker for walking in their magic and inviting me into a world of practice. This book would not be imaginable without "The Betas" (Jessica Hood, Aliya Nealy, Naya Stevens, Tori Lynn Dobbs, Shemira Pennyman, and Solanny Sanchez), who were my Sisterhood during undergrad, who stumbled through survival with me, who teased the seams and held me in the reflections of their laughter. I would not have been brave enough to write this book without the voices of Kesi KMT and Amaris Brown, who each, in their own ways, sat me down and invited me to listen.

This book would not be imaginable without the production of "The Niggas Speak of Rivers," put on by the Destiny Arts Spring 2017 Queer Emerging Artist Residency Cohort (Aurielle Lucier, Kiki Nicole, Sentura Cruz, Umniya Hamden, Mylo Santifer, Miranda Shepard, Tianna Bratcher, Bobbi Kindred, and Davia Amerasu Spain). Your work opened me up to a new way to play with language, a new way to tell the most honest stories, a new way to relate to the blackqueerness of my body's survival. This book would not be imaginable without the space of loving-witness I have cultivated with my kindreds Sophia Smart and Ayana Flewellen.

And while this text is already overflowing with reference to the literary giants of the ever-evolving Black feminist tradition, I owe a particular wellspring of gratitude to Alice Walker and Dr. Doris Diosa Davenport, who embody in their living and model through their writing radical expressions of Southern Black femininity ripe with loving curiosity and unflinching truth-telling.

I love y'all. I appreciate y'all. I thank God for y'all.

Chorus

Brown, Kimberly Juanita. *The Repeating Body: Slavery's Visual Resonance in the Contemporary*. Duke University Press 2015.

Clifton, Lucille. *Next: New Poems*. BOA Editions 1987.

Federici, Silvia. "How the Demonization of 'Gossip' Is Used to Break Women's Solidarity." *Inthesetimes* (blog) January 31, 2019. https://inthesetimes.com/article/21707/the-subversive-feminist-power-of-gossip.

———, *Witches, Witch-Hunting, and Women*. Oakland, CA: PM Press 2018.

Hartman, Saidiya V. Scenes of Subjection: *Terror, Slavery, and Self-Making in Nineteenth-Century America*. New York: Oxford University Press 1997.

Hoodoo Medicine: Gullah Herbal Remedies. Summerhouse Press 1999.

Hurston, Zora Neale. *Mules and Men*. Harper Collins 2009.

Jesús, Aisha M. Beliso-De. *Electric Santería: Racial and Sexual Assemblages of Transnational Religion*. Columbia University Press 2015.

Jones, Gayl. *Hermit-Woman*. Detroit: Broadside Lotus Press 1983.

Kendrick, Dolores. *Why the Woman Is Singing on the Corner: A Verse Narrative*. Peter E. Randall Publisher 2001.

Lester, Julius. *Uncle Remus: The Complete Tales*. New York: Dial Books 1999.

Lorde, Audre. *Zami: A New Spelling of My Name - A Biomythography*. Trumansburg, NY: Crossing Press 1982.

M.D., Bessel van der Kolk. *The Body Keeps the Score: Brain, Mind, and Body in the Healing of Trauma*. Reprint edition. New York, NY: Penguin Books 2015.

Morrison, Toni. *Jazz*. Knopf Doubleday Publishing Group 2007.

Naylor, Gloria. *Mama Day*. Vintage Books 1989.

"Sally's Rape" In *Moon Marked and Touched by Sun: Plays by African-American Women*. New York: Theatre Communications Group 1993.

Shange, Ntozake. *For Colored Girls Who Have Considered Suicide / When the Rainbow Is Enuf*. Rei edition. New York: Scribner 1989.

Shange, Ntozake. "Interview with Toni Morrison." *American Rag* November 1978.

Spillers, Hortense J. "Mama's Baby, Papa's Maybe: An American Grammar Book." *Diacritics* 17, no. 2 (1987): 65–81. https://doi.org/10.2307/464747.

Stallings, L. H. *Mutha Is Half a Word: Intersections of Folklore, Vernacular, Myth, and Queerness in Black Female Culture*. Columbus: Ohio State University Press 2007.

Wolfe, George C. *The Colored Museum*. Grove Press 1988.

Biographical Note

Ra Malika Imhotep is a Black feminist writer and performance artist from Atlanta, Georgia. As a scholar and cultural worker, Ra/Malika is invested in exploring relationships between queer articulations of Black femininity, Southern vernacular culture, and the performance of labor. As a steward of Black Studies and Black feminist thought, Ra/Malika dreams, organizes, and facilitates spaces of critical reflection and embodied spiritual–political education. Ra/Malika is a co-convenor of The Church of Black Feminist Thought and a member of The Black Aesthetic curatorial collective.